Love Your Budgerigar

W0007462

Roy Stringer

W. Foulsham & Co. Ltd.
London • New York • Toronto • Cape Town • Sydney

Page 2: Normal Green Budgerigar

W. Foulsham & Company Limited
Yeovil Road, Slough, Berkshire, SL1 4JH

ISBN 0-572-01240-3

Printed in Spain by Cayfosa. Barcelona
Dep. Leg. B-11516-1986

Contents

1 The Decision to Keep a Budgerigar

So you think you would like to keep a budgerigar? Have you thought what this involves? Keeping a pet of any kind is a responsibility. A budgerigar must be fed and watered every day and cleaned out at least once a week. If you go away on holiday someone has to be found to do these jobs for you. A budgerigar needs a good cage and this will cost money; so will the equipment such as drinkers and feeders.

However, keeping a budgerigar will give you a lot of pleasure. Budgerigars are lively, friendly birds which come to know their owners. They can be taught to talk, if you buy the correct bird in the first place. Some can even remember whole Nursery Rhymes! If you decide to keep several budgerigars you will be able to breed from them and it can turn into an interesting hobby if you go to Bird Shows and meet other budgerigar breeders.

2 Housing a Budgerigar

Whether you are going to buy a pet budgerigar, or more than one for breeding, it is best to have a cage ready for when you arrive home. This will mean that the bird will be put straight into its own home and not be disturbed by being kept in some temporary housing.

If you are going to keep a pet budgerigar in the house there are lots of designs of cage available in pet shops. Nearly all of them will house your budgerigar safely and comfortably. It is best to buy the largest cage that you can afford, remembering that it has to fit in one of your rooms at home. Cages with plastic bottoms, which can be removed, are easily disinfected. Cages with metal bottoms can become rusty after a time. Some pet cages have perches which are too small in diameter. Perches should be no smaller than 12mm (½ inch) diameter. Perches of different sizes, say one 12mm (½ inch) and the other of 15mm (⅝ inch) are ideal. But perches are easily changed, so if you find a cage which suits you, do not be put off by the perches. Change them.

If you want to breed budgerigars you will need a breeding cage. This can be made quite cheaply from plywood and a wire cage front bought from a pet shop. Although some breeders use slightly smaller cages, an ideal size is 76cm long, 46cm high and 38cm from front to back. (2'–6" × 1'–6" × 1'–3"). Even better is a "double breeder". This is a cage fitted with two cage fronts with a small gap between them. A slide can be put in to divide the cage into two, so that two pairs can breed in the same cage. Or one pair can be breeding and other budgerigars — say their first lot of chicks — can be separated. A double-breeder should be at least 122cm long (4'–0") but 152cm (5'–0") would be better.

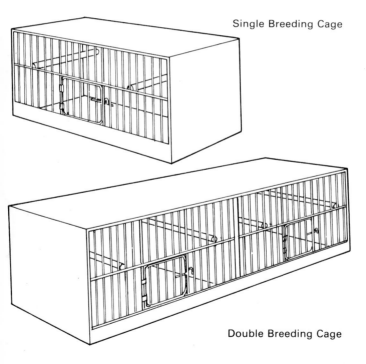

Single Breeding Cage

Double Breeding Cage

Even more attention needs to be paid to perches in a breeding cage. Budgerigars mate on the perch and if a perch is not fixed firmly it can be the cause of infertile eggs. The hen needs to be able to grip the perch during mating and so at least one of the perches should be square in section. A length of wood, 15mm (⅝ inch) square, with the sharp corners removed, serves very well.

If you have a garden an aviary is an ideal place to house and breed budgerigars. The size of aviary will depend on the size of your garden and how many birds you intend to keep. A wooden frame 1.8m. × 1.8m. × 1.2m (6' × 6' × 4') covered with 12mm (½ inch) wire netting will comfortably house six pairs of budgerigars. Welded wire mesh 25mm × 12mm (1 inch × ½ inch) is a good alternative to the netting. 19 gauge (thickness) wire is thick enough, but 16 gauge is better. Always fix the wire to the inside of the wooden frame as this will help to prevent the budgerigars chewing holes in the framing. The birds will also need a waterproof and draughtproof shelter to sleep in. This can form one end of the flight and for the size of aviary described a depth of 0.6m (2') would be large enough. The shelter should have a large door into the flight, which can be opened in hot weather and for cleaning out and a small door 15cm (6 inches) square will do) for the birds to get from the shelter to the flight. Both doors can be closed when the birds have gone inside to roost for the night. The shelter must be fitted with plenty of perches so that every bird can find a place it likes. In the flight, small branches from fruit trees can be used as perching. Do not use the wood

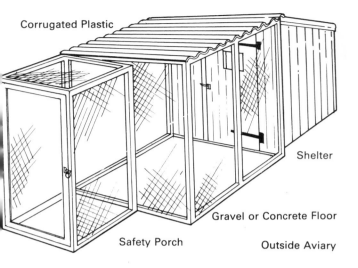

Corrugated Plastic

Shelter

Gravel or Concrete Floor

Safety Porch

Outside Aviary

of other trees. You will need to take care when building the door from the garden into the flight, which you will need to use when you go in to feed, clean out or even just stand admiring your birds. You must make sure that the birds do not fly past you and escape as you are going in. The first rule is that flight doors should always open inwards so that you fill the door opening as you go in. Safest of all is a small wire-mesh covered porch. With this you open a door, step into the porch, close the first door and then open the door into the flight. If you do not have a porch, then a door only about 1m high (3'3") can be used. You will find that as you enter the budgerigars will fly up and away and this will give you time to go in without any escaping.

The roof of the flight should be covered with sheets of corrugated plastic. This will keep out the droppings of wild birds — which could carry disease — and help to protect your budgerigars from cats. Garden soil and lawn are not suitable floors for budgerigar flights. They soon become messy and are very difficult to clean. Best are either concrete or a thick layer of gravel which can be washed with a hose pipe.

Blue

3 **Equipment**

The equipment you need for your cage consists mainly of feeding utensils. You can use dishes and bowls, not made specially for budgerigars, but it is better to use drinkers and feeders which have been specially designed.

If you give water in an open dish it will soon become full of seed husks and droppings, and will not be clean enough for your budgerigar to drink. Your pet will also play in the water at a time when you do not want him to get wet. You also have to open the door to put the water dish into the cage. The best utensil for giving water is a plastic water fountain. This clips on to the outside of the cage, will not fill up with seed husks or droppings and can be changed without opening the cage door. The part of the fountain inside the cage is too small for your budgerigar to be able to bathe when you do not want him to. The open dish, already in the pet cage when you buy it, can be used for grit.

The same type of water fountain can be used on a breeding cage, but if you keep several pairs in a flight you need something which will hold more water. You can buy a galvanised base which holds a plastic lemonade bottle. This is a standard animal drinker.

An open dish is better for seed than for water but still has the problems that droppings

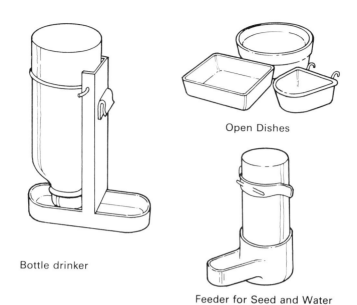

Bottle drinker

Open Dishes

Feeder for Seed and Water

can get in with the seed and the cage door has to be opened for refilling. A larger version of the water fountain can be bought, with the same advantages. When using with seed you should read the instructions carefully. There is a gap in the plastic tube which needs to be lined up with the feeding outlet so that the seed can flow freely. In breeding cages and flights you may need something larger. There are many types of seed hopper on the market. One which works well with budgerigars has a plastic base on which you can stand a glass jar. It is best to buy a clip to hold a piece of cuttle fish bone which budgerigars like to eat. This stops the bone getting dirty by lying around on the cage floor.

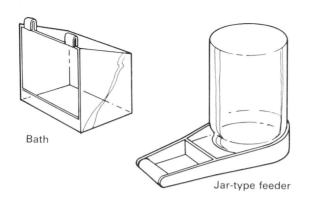

Bath

Jar-type feeder

Budgerigars love to take a bath. Specially designed baths can be bought from pet shops which fit over the cage door opening. The advantage of these is that you can decide the best time for your pet to bathe and the rest of the cage does not get wet.

Although not essential, toys can keep budgerigars happy when you are not at home. Pet shops stock a wide range of toys which includes ladders, mirrors and bells. You will be able to choose the toys you think your pet will like best – but do not put too many in the cage at one time or the cage will become overcrowded.

Budgerigars in flights will find plenty to do, particularly if you have used fruit tree branches as perches. But they will still like to play on a swing. A budgerigar which plays is a happy budgerigar.

4 **Selecting the Variety**

When deciding which variety of budgerigar to buy it is really a matter of which colour you like. Unlike some other animals and birds, all varieties of budgerigar are more or less the same size. If you see a budgerigar which is larger than others it will be because it has been bred by someone who shows his birds and has chosen big birds to breed from.

When the first budgerigar was brought to Britain from Australia, nearly 150 years ago it had a bright green body, yellow and black wings and head and a dark blue tail. At that time all budgerigars were that variety, which has become known as Light Green. Since then, breeders all over the world have bred many new coloured varieties. Although some people set out to breed a new colour, it is really a matter of luck. The skill comes from seeing that a new colour has been bred and then choosing a breeding mate to make certain that the colour is not lost.

When choosing a budgerigar as a pet there are far more important things to consider than the variety and these are explained in Chapter 5. There is no truth in the story that some varieties of budgerigar are easier to teach to talk than others. It is all a matter of which colour and markings you like best, although you may have to pay a little more for a brighter coloured bird. You will see a range of varieties in pet shops, but the best place to see the largest number is at a budgerigar show.

The following information will help you to identify some of the varieties of budgerigar:

Greens

All colours of budgerigar come in at least three shades. The first budgerigars to be bought from Australia were Light Greens. The name describes the brightness of their body feathers very well. In the course of breeding with Light Greens it was noticed that a bird with a darker body had been bred, although it still had the same yellow and black markings on wings and head. For a time this new colour was called Laurel Green, but it is now known as Dark Green. Pairing Dark Greens together produced chicks, some of which were even darker in body colour. These became known as Olives. Light Greens, Dark Greens and Olives all have dark blue tails and small patches on their faces – known as cheek patches – which are bright violet.

Even later, another, duller green budgerigar was bred. This is called the Grey Green. Grey Greens have black tails and grey cheek patches.

Blues

When blue budgerigars were first bred they were sold at very high prices but blue budgerigars are no more difficult to breed than any other colour and so their value soon came down. The lightest of the blues is called the

The head of a young
cock budgerigar

Normal Blue (Violet)

17

Skyblue and has body feathers which are a pale turquoise blue. Normal blue budgerigars have black and white wings, white faces and black and white heads. The next darkest blue is called Cobalt and is a rich, attractive colour. Almost like the Cobalt is the Violet in depth of colour but the Violet has an extra sparkle which makes it the most beautiful budgerigar of all. The darkest blue is the Mauve. The Mauve budgerigar may sound attractive but in fact it can appear as a muddy coloured bird.

In with the blue series of budgerigars are the Greys. Greys have the same head and wing markings as blues, but their body feathering is an even Grey colour.

Yellowfaces

Although Normal Blues and Greys have white faces there are varieties called Yellowfaced Blue and Yellowfaced Grey. As the names suggest these have the same colouring as Blues and Greys but with yellow faces. Sometimes the yellow spills on to the body feathers causing interesting shades.

Cinnamons

The Cinnamon factor is mainly to do with the colour of the wing and head markings. Where Normal birds have black markings, Cinnamons have brown markings. A side-effect is that body colour is paler and softer. Cinnamons can be bred in any colour.

Greywings

Like the Cinnamon, the Greywing factor

Yellow-faced Budgerigar

changes the colour of wing and head markings; this time from black to grey. The body colour is pale and soft. Greywings can be bred in any colour.

Opalines

The Opaline factor takes away the black markings from the head and so leaves it plain yellow or white. The wing markings remain black, but the background colour, instead of being yellow or white, is the same colour as the body. So an Opaline Dark Green has black and dark green wings and an Opaline Violet has black and violet wings. The body colour remains as the Normal, if not a little brighter.

Opaline Cinnamons and Opaline Greywings

When Opaline is combined with Cinnamon or Greywing the resulting bird takes its colour distribution from the Opaline factor and the colouring itself from the Cinnamon or Greywing factor. So an Opaline Cinnamon Grey has a white head, with hardly any markings, a pale grey body and pale grey and brown wings.

Yellow-Wings

Yellow-wings have body colours the same depth as normal Green budgerigars. Their wings should be clear yellow, but they usually have light grey markings. They can be bred in any of the Green varieties and look best when of the darker varieties. Yellow-wing Dark Greens have a lovely contrast between their bodies and wings.

Normal Cinnamon

Whitewings

Whitewings have body colours the same depth as normal Blues. Their wings should be pure white, but they usually have pale grey markings. They can be bred in any of the Blue varieties. It has been said that the Whitewing Violet is the most beautiful budgerigar of all.

Rainbows

When the Whitewing, Yellowface and Opaline factors are combined on one bird, it is called a Rainbow. Some people call any very brightly coloured budgerigar a "Rainbow", but the true Rainbow is a Yellowfaced Opaline Whitewing Blue.

Albinos

Albinos are pure white budgerigars with pink eyes. In some lights, on some birds, you can see a pale blue sheen on the rump and under the vent. Albinos are always of the Blue series and so can be bred with Yellow Faces. When the yellow spills on to the body a delicately coloured lemon shade results.

Lutinos

Lutinos are bred from the same factor as Albinos but are of the Green series. They are pure yellow with pink eyes. The depth of colour varies from bird to bird and hens tend to be paler than cocks.

Lacewings

Lacewings are a fairly new variety of budgeri-

Opaline Dark Green

gar. They are best described as looking like Lutinos and Albinos with Cinnamon wing markings. They are not always easy to obtain, but there are breeders who specialise in the variety.

Pieds

Pied budgerigars are very attractive and all over the world there are clubs for people who keep Pieds. The main effect the Pied factor has is to put patches of clear colour on to an otherwise normal bird. On a Green Pied you will see yellow feathers on the body, clear yellow patches on the wings and some have clear yellow tails and a yellow spot on the back of the head. Blue Pieds have clear patches which are white in colour. There is more than one type of Pied and each type has different markings. Recessive Pieds usually have more clear feathers than Dominant Pieds.

Spangles

The newest variety to become available is the Spangle. This has the colouring of a Normal but with the wing markings reversed. So where a Normal has black on its wings, the Spangle has yellow or white and where the Normal has yellow or white, the Spangle has black. Surprisingly, such a simple change has produced a strikingly beautiful budgerigar. In some countries Spangles are still quite rare and might be difficult to obtain. If available they are likely to be more expensive than other varieties.

Crested

Crested Budgerigars have longer feathers on

Opaline Cinnamon Grey

top of their heads. The crest can be anything between a small tuft on the front of the head and a full circle of long feathers. As yet, budgerigar crests have not been developed to the same extent as on some varieties of Canary. Because of the factors which control the crest, only a small proportion of the chicks bred from crests carry a crest themselves. This means that it is not always easy to buy a Crested Budgerigar.

Whitewing Blue

5 Buying a Budgerigar

Before going out to buy a budgerigar, you should make up your mind where your interest lies. Do you want a friendly pet, which will learn to talk? Or do you want to breed these beautiful little parakeets?

If it is a pet you want, you must buy a young cock bird which is still in its baby feathering. Hens will learn to talk, but cocks are much easier to teach. If you buy from an experienced pet shop owner or an established breeder of budgerigars he or she will be almost certain which chicks are cocks and which are hens. If a mistake is made, many breeders will be willing to exchange your chick for another. They usually prefer to keep more hens than cocks.

What to look for when buying a pet budgerigar

When you think you have found the budgerigar you would like as a pet, take a good look at it and check out several things.

1. Is the bird a young cock?
   Young budgies do not have a white ring around the eye. This makes them look wide-

eyed and cuddly. On many varieties the black or brown lines, seen on the back of an adults head, come right to the front of the head. For this reason, young budgerigars are known as Bar Heads. Some young birds have black, or dark brown, beaks. The fleshy part, just above the beak, is known as the Cere. It is the colour of the cere which shows whether a budgerigar is a cock or a hen. The cere of a young cock shows a purplish-pink tinge. A young hen's cere is more white, with either a biscuit or a pale blue tinge. Because an adult cock bird's cere is blue, many people make the mistake of thinking that a blue tinge on a very young budgerigar's cere means that it is a cock.

2. Is it healthy?
   A bird which looks happy and bright, moving about busily, is a fit bird. A wide-open bright eye is another good sign. Any bird which sits quietly, with its eyes partly closed and feathers fluffed up, should not be bought.

3. Is the beak properly formed?
   If the lower part of the beak overlaps the upper (undershot) or the upper part looks too long (overshot) choose another bird. These conditions can cause difficulty in eating and — if you decide to use the bird for breeding at a later date — they can be passed on to chicks.

4. Does the beak look shiny?
   Any bird with a crusty look to its beak could be suffering from Scaly Face and is best avoided. The bird you buy should have clean, shiny beak.

5. Are the feathers under the vent clean?

Rainbow Budgerigar (Yellowfaced Opaline Whitewing Blue)

If a bird has dirty vent feathers it may have a stomach upset. It is best left and another one chosen.

What to look for when buying budgerigars to breed

If you are buying budgerigars to breed from, it is best to choose cocks and hens which are about twelve months old and have never been used for breeding. Birds more than two years old should not be bought. When birds are bought from a breeder who shows his budgerigars, you can get a good idea of their ages. The year each bird was bred is stamped on the aluminium ring on its leg. When you buy unringed adult budgerigars, you cannot tell their ages.

Signs of old-age are very scaly legs on both cocks and hens and very nobbly, dark brown ceres on hens. A cock with an almost black cere should not be bought. This can show that a bird is too old to breed. All of the health checks when buying a pet budgerigar (2 to 6) also apply to breeding birds. You should also check —

a) Is the bird the sex you want?
A cock bird should have a bright blue cere. The exceptions to this rule are the pure white and pure yellow varieties of budgerigar (Albinos and Lutinos). Even as adults, the cocks of these varieties have ceres which are more purplish-pink than blue.

According to the stage of the breeding condition cycle, a hen's cere will vary

Albino

Lutino

between a pale biscuit colour and deep brown. This is also true of Albino and Lutino hens.

b) Is a hen able to lay eggs?
Hens which have been used for breeding sometimes develop a large, fatty lump under the vent. Hens like this cannot lay eggs and so should not be bought.

6 Food and Water

Seed

The basic food a budgerigar needs is a mixture of plain canary seed and millets. The seeds come from all over the world and this helps to make sure that there is everything in the seed to make a budgerigar strong and fit. When you look at a mixed seed, you will see a brown seed which is pointed at both ends. This is canary seed. Millets are usually round in shape and come in various colours and sizes. Pearl white millet is large and white. Panicum millet is small and yellow. Japanese millet is brown and Dakota millet is red.

There is no need to worry about the details of each seed. You can buy a Budgerigar Mixture to suit your birds. For a single pet bird you can buy packets of seed. If you have more birds it is usually cheaper to buy loose seed from a pet shop. Usually the more you buy at one time, the less it will cost you to feed your budgerigars.

When your birds are breeding it is best to increase the amount of plain canary seed in the mixture. A budgerigar needs to have seed available at all times.

Water

A budgerigar needs to have clean drinking

water available at all times. From time to time you can add a vitamin additive or tonic to the drinking water. These can be bought from good pet shops. When adding anything to your budgerigars' water always read the instructions carefully and do not add more than the stated amount. Budgerigars are small birds and require only small amounts of additives.

Grit

Budgerigars need a supply of grit so that they can digest their food. When they eat seeds, they remove the husk and swallow the kernel whole. A store of grit, kept in the crop, grinds up the seeds before they pass further into the digestive system. Grit comes in the form of Mineral Grit and Oystershell Grit. Both work equally well. It is thought that grit which is too sharp can damage the inside of a budgerigar's crop and so it is best to buy a good brand which has been specially prepared for budgerigars.

Cuttlefish Bone

Budgerigars like to chew at a piece of cuttlefish bone. They benefit from the calcium they consume as this helps to make their bones strong. Breeding hens need calcium to form the shells of the eggs they lay.

Iodine Block

Iodine blocks can be bought from pet shops, ready to fix on to the wires of the cage. By chewing the block your budgerigar will benefit from iodine and minerals which will help to keep it healthy.

Greenfood

Budgerigars love to eat greenfood but you must be very careful when feeding it. The cheapest form of greenfood is dandelion leaves and chickweed but there is a risk involved when using these. If wild greens have been sprayed, to kill weeds or insects, they can be dangerous to feed to your budgerigar. There is also a risk that a dog or cat has used the ground around the weeds as a toilet. Any greens should be washed and dried before feeding to your birds. So it is best to feed greens which you grow yourself or buy at a greengrocers. Lettuce, spinach and cress are suitable. Greens should be fed early in the day and in small quantities. They are absorbed quickly into the digestive system and if fed in the evening can lead to a bird spending the night with an empty crop. The remains of greens should be removed from the cage the same day that they are given to avoid the eating of stale food. Greens can be fed two or three times a week.

Treats

As well as their basic diet budgerigars love to sample all sorts of food. Perhaps the best known is the Millet Spray. Millet Sprays should be looked upon as a treat as budgerigars can get on very well without them, but some would eat nothing else if given the chance. A spray can be very useful to give to a budgerigar which looks a little off colour, but can make a bird fat.

Small slices of carrot or fresh fruit, such as sweet apple or orange, are good for budgerigars. Any left over should be removed from the cage the same day. Although some budgerigars will eat almost anything, there are foods which are best avoided if your bird is not to get too fat. Such foods are bread, cake and biscuits. The exception to this is when feeding hens, which themselves are feeding chicks. Then, bread and milk is an ideal food.

To sum up: a budgerigar must have seed, water and grit available all of the time. Care should be taken when feeding extra food as this can make your budgerigar fat. A fat bird is not a fit bird.

7 General Management and Training

The management of a budgerigar – or several budgerigars – is very simple. It need take only a few minutes each day, with an extra effort once a week when cleaning out. This means that, when you buy a budgerigar, you will be able to look after it properly and still have plenty of time to enjoy its company.

You need to find a good position for your budgerigar's cage. A cool, airy place is best, so avoid draughts and direct sunshine. This means that placing a cage in a window is *not* a good idea. Being placed in a draught can cause your budgerigar to become ill.

The position of seed and water feeders is also important. Seed and water must never be placed in a position where your bird's droppings can get into them. Under a perch is the *worst* possible place. The same is true of any other item you put into the cage such as cuttlefish bone, millet sprays, greens, fruit and even toys. Find a position where they will stay clean.

Both seed and water need your attention every day. The water container should be washed and then rinsed thoroughly, before being refilled with fresh water. When a fountain type feeder is used for seed it should be checked every day to see that there is plenty of seed inside and that the outlet for the seed is not blocked. Seed husks are not usually a problem with this type of feeder. If it looks as though the level of seed has not gone down, check at once. This can mean that there is a blockage and that your budgerigar cannot get at its seed.

When seed is fed in an open dish the empty seed husks tend to lie on top. These need to be blown off every day, taking care not get a seed husk in your eye. When the seed husks are gone you will be able to see how much seed is left in the dish. Even then, check once more as sometimes you will find a layer of dust in the bottom of the dish. Fill up the seed dish every day. And remember finally, your pet budgerigar will sleep better if you place a piece of light cloth over its cage late in the evening.

Training

Budgerigars kept in breeding cages and flights do not need training. But a lot of the pleasure of keeping a pet budgerigar is seeing how easy it is to train.

First you need to gain the pet's confidence and, although you may find it difficult, you must leave the bird alone for the first day after you have put it into the cage. This will give it time to settle down after all of the upset of being moved. It may sit quietly at first but as it becomes more sure of itself it will investigate the cage and start to chirp. When you go to the cage say the same two words, quietly, over and over again. If you are good at training,

Lacewing

these will be the first two words your pet will say. "Hallo," followed by its name, or "Pretty Boy" are good starter words.

When you are sure that your pet is not afraid of you, gently open the cage door and slowly put your hand into the cage. If the bird panics, slowly remove your hand, close the door and wait until it settles down before trying again. When the bird accepts your hand in its cage, extend your first finger and place it gently against its chest. You may find that your budgerigar will step on to your finger at this point. If it does not, then press your finger gently against the bird's chest. This almost always causes it to step on to your finger. Still moving very slowly, gently transfer your pet to another perch. It will soon get used to this and know what to expect when next you do it.

When your budgerigar has learned this lesson well, you can try bringing it out of the cage. But before doing so there are several things to check to make sure that it will be safe. Make sure that all doors and windows are closed. If you have an open fireplace, make sure that it is guarded. Pull the curtain across any clear glass windows, or your pet, not knowing that there is any glass there, will fly into it and may damage itself. If you have a cat or dog make sure that they are not in the room. When your bird flies around the room watch what it is doing as budgerigars will chew papers and house plants if left to do it.

If your budgerigar has learned its lesson well, you should have no difficulty getting it back into its cage. Just follow the method used when training to get it on to your finger and put your hand back into the cage. If it forgets

Dominant Pied

40

its training and refuses to come to your hand you have more of a problem. First darken the room, which will permit you to get close, without your pet flying off. Then throw a soft cloth over it to capture it. When handling a budgerigar, always hold its wings firmly to its body, in their natural position. You must be firm enough to prevent the bird hurting itself, but not so firm as to hurt it yourself. By placing your thumb on one side of the budgerigar's face, your forefinger on the back of its head and your second finger on the other side of its face, with the wings and body in the palm of your hand, you will be holding the bird safely. Then return it to the cage. Carry on training your pet to stand on your finger until you can return it to the cage without capturing it.

When your budgerigar is standing on your finger see if it will let you gently stroke its head and beak. If it does, your training is going well. Always move slowly and gently as if you frighten your pet it will take much longer for it to become tame. Repeating the same two word phrase over and over again, to reassure your budgerigar, will have made a start to teaching it to talk. Do not change the words until it has learned to say the first two. The more often you repeat the words the quicker your pet will learn them. Once it has learned the first words you can start teaching another two. If you are a good teacher it will not be long before your budgerigar knows lots of words. Some birds can repeat complete nursery rhymes – although they do get mixed up sometimes – which makes everyone laugh.

8 Cleaning Out

Any pet needs to be cleaned out regularly. It depends on you to keep its housing and equipment clean. Budgerigars need to be cleaned out at least once a week. You can buy sand paper sheets from a pet shop which make cleaning out very simple, as far as the floor of the cage is concerned. It is just a matter of removing the old sheet and putting a new sheet in its place. Budgerigars often chew these sand sheets. This does them no harm. It is a little cheaper to use bird sand on the floor of a cage, but it will take a little more time to remove the sand and to replace it.

In breeding cages, wood shavings are often used to cover the cage floor. These are not so good in pet cages as they tend to come out of the cage when the budgerigar flutters its wings. If you do decide to use wood shavings, buy them from a pet shop. Shavings bought from a wood yard may have been treated with chemicals which could make your bird ill. The cheapest of all cage floor coverings is a piece of newspaper. This works well but does not look as attractive as the others.

About once a month you should disinfect the cage and equipment. Use a mild disinfectant and rinse feeders and water containers well in clean water before refilling them. Disinfectant should be used more often if a budgerigar has a stomach upset and its droppings are green instead of the normal black and white. Perches need special attention when cleaning out. They can become very dirty with the birds own droppings which, if left, get hard and could damage a budgerigar's feet. Perches should be scrubbed with disinfectant, rinsed and dried before being put back in the cage.

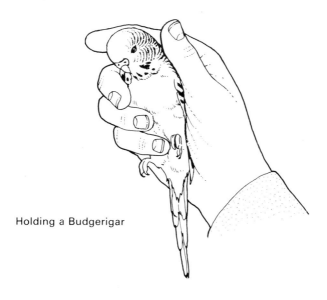

Holding a Budgerigar

9 **Illness and Disease**

Budgerigars are hardy little birds which can stand a wide range of conditions without becoming ill. Some item of food, causing a stomach upset, or being placed in a draught, bringing on a cold, are the most usual causes of illness. They are naturally bright, active birds and so the first sign of illness can be that they sleep longer than is usual. A small change to the diet or position of the cage at this stage can stop the illness going any further. But if your budgerigar reaches the stage where it is huddled up on the floor of the cage it is time to get the advice of a vet.

Enteritis

Stomach upsets are the most common form of illness in budgerigars. The appearance of the bird and its droppings are both signs that a budgerigar is suffering from enteritis. A slight case will see a budgerigar sitting quietly, feathers fluffed up rather than smooth, sleeping more than usual with its head under its wing and its droppings will be green rather than the normal black and white. In a severe case the fluffing up will be to the point where the bird's head seems to be withdrawn into its body and its eyes will be closed. The bird's droppings will be coating its vent and tail.

The first step in treating any case of stomach upset is to move the bird to a warm place and remove any food other than the seed mixture. Green food is often the cause of enteritis, particularly if it is stale, dirty, wet or has been subject to frost. So make sure that your bird eats no green food while it is ill. Even when your bird is well all green food should be taken from the cage at the end of each day so that it cannot be eaten when it is stale. Pet shops sell medicines which can be put in a budgerigar's drinking water. In slight cases of stomach upsets, one of these can be tried for a couple of days. If the bird gets not better then you should consult a vet. In serious cases it is best to speak to a vet straight away.

Sickness

Sickness, like enteritis, is caused by a stomach upset but results in a bird bringing up the contents of its stomach through the beak. This clings, in a sticky mess, to the face and head of a budgerigar. Because it is a stomach upset, treatment begins as it did for enteritis. Keep the bird warm and take away all food except the seed. Make sure that the bird has no green food to eat. Try a medicine, from a pet shop, at first, but if the bird is no better after a couple of days consult a vet. If, at any stage, the bird becomes more ill, speak to a vet at once.

You should not make the mistake of mixing up sickness with breeding fitness in cock budgerigars. Cock budgerigars feed their mates when they are ready to breed. They bring up pieces of seed and, if there is not a hen in the

Recessive Pied

cage, will try to feed them to a mirror or other toy. This is called "regurgitation". When a bird is sick, the food it brings up is wet and sometimes has an unpleasant smell.

Moult

Moulting cannot be called an illness as it is just a case of a bird dropping its old feathers so that it can grow new ones. In the wild this happens once a year, but the changes of temperature, in a house, can cause it to happen more often. A bird which is moulting is more liable to become ill and so it should be kept in a temperature as constant as possible. A tonic in the drinking water helps a budgerigar when it is moulting.

French Moult

If you have a young budgerigar which has lost all, or most, of its large wing and tail feathers it could well be suffering from French Moult. If you look closely at the quill in the centre of a French Moulter's large feathers you will see dried blood inside the quill. Although there are many theories, no-one really knows what causes French Moult. The birds themselves do not seem to suffer at all and run and climb instead of flying. Because they cannot fly, French Moulters often make good pets and many recover their feathers when they moult into adult plumage.

Feather Plucking

There are two types of feather plucking. The plucking of other birds' feathers — usually a

mother pulling the feathers out of her chicks —
and cases of budgerigar plucking their own
feathers. Budgerigars in flights will always
swing by the beak from other birds' tails and
often the tails come out. This is not feather
plucking, it is budgerigars at play.

Hens in nest boxes sometimes start pulling
out feathers from their chicks' heads. What
starts as a show of affection can become more
serious when a hen wants the chicks to leave
the nest so that she can lay another clutch of
eggs. A cream can be bought, to be rubbed
on the chicks' heads, which helps to stop the
hen plucking and moving the chicks out of the
box, on to the cage floor, can help. Feathers
plucked from the head usually grow back in.
Those taken from the wings often grow in
unevenly. Hens which feather pluck should
not be used for breeding again; nor should the
young hens bred from them. Many people
think that feather plucking is an inherited habit.
When a bird starts to pull out its own feathers it
is almost certainly due to one of two causes; a
feather mite or stress.

No matter what the cause it pays to treat for
mite. Pet shops sell powders and sprays which
can be used both on birds and equipment. If
the cause is a mite it can be cured quickly in
this way. Stress is more difficult. If a budgerigar becomes so bored that it sits and pulls out
its own feathers you must find a way of keeping it occupied. Toys of all sorts can be bought
at pet shops. Try one at a time to see if you can
find what sort of plaything your pet likes. A
mirror works well, as it makes the bird think
that there is another bird in its cage. Changing
the position of the cage can help, even to the

point of moving it to another room where the bird will get more company. When a budgerigar is left alone during the day, leave a radio playing quietly to keep it company. As a last resort, buy a second budgerigar, but it is possible that they will not get on together and there is a good chance that the arrival of another bird will stop your pet from talking.

Scaly Face

A budgerigar which has a crusty look to its beak and cere is most probably suffering from Scaly Face. This is caused by a mite which burrows below the surface and, if left untreated, spreads to the legs and around the eyes. Scaly face can spread very quickly through an aviary but can be cured in a few days with a cream or liquid, bought from a pet shop.

Beaks and Claws

Sometimes a budgerigar's beak or claws can become overgrown. Cuttlefish bone and iodine nibbles help to keep beaks trimmed. Some pet shops sell perches with sandpaper fixed to the underside. These can help to keep claws the correct length.

The cutting of beaks and claws is best left to experts. At the centre of claws and beaks are blood vessels and cutting by an inexperienced person can cause bleeding to occur. If you do cut a claw, check where the blood vessel stops – by holding up to the light – and cut no closer than 3mm (⅛ inch) to this.

Spangle Blue

Half-sider-
a rarity

51

Egg Binding

Occasionally, when breeding, a budgerigar hen becomes egg bound. All hens become swollen under the vent when they are laying and this should not be confused with egg binding. If a hen looks bright and alert it is *not* egg bound. An egg bound hen looks fluffed up and unwell; often sitting on the floor of the cage. Keeping the hen warm is often all that is required for it to pass the egg. A little olive oil brushed on to the vent opening helps. As a last resort the hen can be held over a cup of hot water so that the steam can relax the vent. Be very careful not to let the hen be scalded. If possible, the advice of an experienced breeder of budgerigars should be sought.

Injuries

Injuries, such as broken legs and wings, should be treated as quickly as possible by a vet.

General

Never be afraid to ask the advice of an experienced breeder if you are worried that your budgerigar might be ill. When giving medicine in the drinking water always make sure that the dose is that stated on the bottle and take away any other drinking water.

10 **Breeding**

Budgerigars will breed at any time of the year
if they are fit and given the correct conditions.
This is because in the wild they are triggered
to breed not by the season of the year but by
water being available. Even in the deserts of
Australia, rain means that grasses will begin to
grow. By going to nest when it rains, budgerigars know that there will be food for their
chicks by the time they hatch.

If you wish to breed your budgerigars in
winter you should be prepared to provide ar-
tificial lighting so that there are twelve hours
in which the parents can feed their chicks. Heat
is not required as long as the temperature in
the room where the breedng cage is housed
remains above 4.5°C (40°F). Breeding budgerigars in open flights is best left until spring
brings warmer weather and longer days.

You can get some idea of whether your
budgerigars are fit to breed from the colour of
their ceres (the fleshly part just above the
beak). But the way the birds are behaving is a
better indication. When fit for breeding a cock
budgerigar's cere will be bright blue; a hen's
will be changing from a biscuit colour to a rich
brown. Both sexes will be active: the cocks
chattering and flying about all of the time: the
hens spending their time chewing wood.

Normally, budgerigars will not breed if there

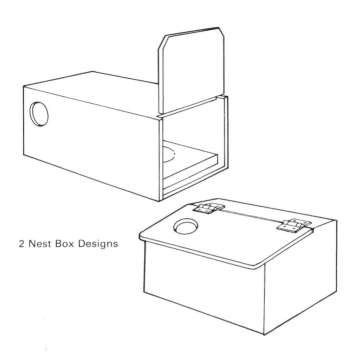

2 Nest Box Designs

is a single pair, so be prepared to keep two or more pairs if you want them to breed. Budgerigars should not be allowed to breed if they are younger than ten months old. In the wild, when they are ready to breed, budgerigars find holes in trees and among the roots in which to nest. They do not build nests like many other birds. The hens chew the wood to form it into a shape to suit them and often lay their eggs on the wood chips they produce.

All you need to do to start your budgerigars breeding – assuming they are fit – is to give them a nest box. Budgerigars will nest happily in a plywood box 23cm long, 15cm wide and

15cm high. (9 × 6 × 6 inches). They will not mind if the box is a little larger and detail design is not important. In the past budgerigars have used coconut shells and cardboard boxes as nests! In the bottom of the box it is best to have a block of wood, about 2cm (¾") thick with a slight hollow at one end so that the eggs will roll to the bottom of the hollow and not be spread all around the box. This is called a "concave". The box will need a hole cut in it, about 5cm (2 inches) in diameter, so that the hen can get in and out. The last thing that is needed is a door for you to be able to look in, to check that everything is going well.

When breeding in cages, nest boxes can be placed either inside the cage or mounted on the outside, with a hole in the cage lined up with the entrance hole in the box. It is best to have only one pair of birds in each cage, as, in a confined space, hens may fight because they both want the same box. Some fighting can take place when breeding in flights but the extra space helps and there are ways to avoid problems. You should always put more nest boxes in the flight than there are hens. The nest boxes should all be at the same height, preferably high up. It is best to have an equal number of cocks and hens. If, in spite of all your precautions, fighting does take place you should watch to see which hen is the trouble-maker. The offender should be removed from the flight; possibly to breed in a cage. Be careful not to be too hasty as there will always be squabbling when several pairs of birds are breeding in the same aviary. There is a difference between squabbling and fighting.

You will find that cocks and hens will soon

pair off. A cock will feed a hen and both will chase off other birds – usually cocks – who try to interrupt the courtship. This is when extra cock birds in a flight become a nuisance. They do not have mates of their own and so try to attract hens away from their chosen partners.

As a cock feeds a hen you will see him tap her beak, chattering all of the time. When mating is going to take place, the hen crouches on the perch and forms her back into a hollow. The cock steps on to the hen's back, places one wing across her neck, tucks his tail under her vent and mating takes place. Eggs are fertilised by the cock bird spraying sperm on to the hen's vent. Firmly fixed perches are essential if a mating is to be successful.

11 **Eggs and Chicks**

Once a hen has started to go into a nest box regularly, it will be about ten to fourteen days before the first egg is laid. The signs that a hen is going to lay are the vent area becomes swollen, her tail pumps up and down and her droppings increase greatly in quantity and become wet.

A handful of clean sawdust, placed in the bottom of the nest box concave, will show if the hen has been in the box or not. Some hens do not like sawdust and throw it out on to the cage floor. Others accept the sawdust and lay their eggs on it. This is better, as the sawdust keeps the eggs clean and stops them rolling around each time the hen leaves the nest box. Once a hen has started laying she will lay an egg every other day. So after three days there will be two eggs, after five days there will be three eggs and so on. A clutch of budgerigar eggs can vary from one to ten, but around six is normal.

It is the hen budgerigar which sits on the eggs, but some cock birds join their mate in the nest box. It takes eighteen days of the hen sitting on the eggs (incubation) for them to hatch. Because the eggs have been laid every other day, the chicks will hatch every other day. Sometimes a hen does not begin sitting until she has laid the second egg. Then the first two chicks hatch on the same day – twenty days after the first egg was laid. Because of this staggered laying and hatching, the first chick is often seven days old by the time the fourth chick hatches.

When a budgerigar egg is laid it is creamy white in colour. If it is not fertile it stays that colour and you can see through the shell if the egg is held in front of a bright light. If the egg is fertile the yolk moves to the rounder end of the egg and after four days blood vessels can be seen forming as the chick develops through its first stages. Two days later, a fertile egg looks like a shiny white pebble.

Although you can open the nest box door once a day, to see that everything is going well, you should not interfere more than this. If a hen lets an egg get cold, during its eighteen days of incubation, the partly formed chick inside may die. The egg is then known as an addled egg and will change colour from a clear white and take on a brown tinge.

Some hours before an egg is due to hatch the chick can be heard calling, still inside the shell. When a chick is newly hatched it has a small "horn" on its top beak. It is with this horn that it chips its way out of the shell. It pokes a small hole, turns a little, pokes again and goes on doing this until the end of the shell drops away, allowing the chick to leave the shell. If a chick does not succeed in getting out of the shell and dies in the attempt, it is known as "dead-in-shell".

Within a few hours of hatching, a chick will have been fed by its mother. Hearing the chick, calling from within the egg, starts the hen to produce a milk like substance in her crop. At first it is this crop milk only which is fed to chicks, but as they get older solid seed is fed as well until at three weeks old chicks are fed seed only. Budgerigar chicks are fed while they are lying on their backs. Their beaks open and the hen puts in the food which she has already partly digested in her crop. As the chicks grow larger some nest boxes become quite dirty. Changing the sawdust every week helps to keep the chicks' feet clean. Many hens who do not like sawdust when they are laying eggs, accept it when there are chicks in the nest.

If a chick's feet become caked in droppings, never try to remove the dirt by picking it off with your fingers. You could easily damage the partly formed feet. Instead, soak the feet in warm water and remove the droppings when they have become soft.

If you are going to exhibit your budgerigars you may put closed aluminium rings on each chick at about ten days old. You should check each day that the ring is clean and that there is no sawdust, seed or droppings trapped between the ring and the chick's leg. Chicks leave the nest box when they are about five weeks old. The cock bird can be seen teaching each chick how to eat and how to fly. Very occasionally, when a chick is bigger than its nest mates, a cock bird can mistake it for another cock bird and attack it. Although this is unusual, it is as well to have a small box ready — like a small nest box — so that it can be put on the cage floor with the chicks inside. The cock will feed the chicks but if he tries to attack them they can go to the back of the box.

When you are sure that the chicks are feeding themselves they can be moved to another cage. Even then it is a good idea to put a friendly cock bird with them. He may help them feed and will teach them how to behave sensibly. By this time the hen will have started laying another clutch of eggs. Two nests of eggs and chicks are enough if the chicks are to be strong and healthy. As long as there is a nest box available, budgerigars will carry on breeding until they lose their fitness, so to stop them breeding, remove the nest box.

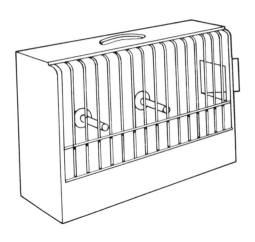

Standard Show Cage

12 **Showing Budgerigars**

If you are interested in budgerigars, other than as a pet, a bird show is the place to go. Some shows are advertised in local newspapers, but to find out what clubs and shows are in your area you should buy *Cage and Aviary Birds* magazine. This is a weekly paper which deals with all aspects of bird keeping and carries news of club meetings and shows.

Once you have located your local cage bird society or budgerigar society you may choose to join. By comparing your budgerigars with other members' you will get some idea whether your birds are the type which can win prizes. The larger the show you go to, the wider the varieties of budgerigar you will see. You will notice that the birds are in good feather condition. Breeders go to a lot of trouble to make sure that their budgerigars are in perfect feather for a show. No judge will give a prize to a bird whose feathers are dirty and uneven.

The Budgerigar Society lays down the show rules and sets a standard for what the 'ideal budgerigar' should look like. It is with this standard in mind that budgerigars are judged. By joining the Budgerigar Society, or one of its ten Area Societies, you will be able to buy aluminium rings which are stamped with your own membership number, the year and a different number for each bird. The colour of these rings is changed each year, so you can tell at a glance the age of a close-ringed budgerigar. Large shows are divided into Sections: Champion, Intermediate, Novice, Beginner and Junior. The Junior section is for young people, under the age of 16, who do not live in the same house as an older person who shows budgerigars. If you are over sixteen years of age you will start by showing your birds in the Beginner Section. There are rules which decide when you must move up to Novice, but, generally, a successful Beginner will move to Novice after three years, to Intermediate after another three years and to Champion after another four years.

After ten years, if you are a Champion, you can apply to the Budgerigar Society to be put on the list of Open Show judges. Within each Section there are classes for each variety and colour of budgerigar. These are split into two groups: Any Age and Breeders. To be shown in the Breeder classes a budgerigar must be entered by the person who bred it and be wearing that person's official closed ring. All other Budgerigars, wearing a ring or not, bred by any breeder, no matter how old, can be shown in the Any Age classes. By winning certain prizes at top level shows, a bird can become a Champion Budgerigar. The budgerigar show season runs from July to November. If you decide to enter a show, you must obtain a standard show cage. All of the cages at a show are the same so that no budgerigar gains an advantage. Club shows, staged just for club members, are usually easy going affairs, where you can turn up with your birds on the day to enter them. The Show Secretary will help you to enter them into the correct classes. Open Shows are more formal and your birds need to be entered in advance. When you find a show you would like to show at, send for a schedule. Ask an experienced breeder for help on which classes your birds should be entered in. Otherwise you may arrive at the show, after judging, to see "W/C" written on your cage. This means "wrong class" and that the bird has not been judged. A few days before the show your cage labels will arrive through the post. Make sure that you stick the correct label to the correct cage before taking your budgerigars to the show hall. The schedule will show what time your birds need to be delivered for judging. It will also show what time the show opens to the public, so that you can return to see if your birds have won.

Better still, ask if you can help at the show, when you send in your entry form. If you do, you must be prepared for hard work, but the whole day will be spent with, and talking about, budgerigars. What better way is there to spend a day?

I hope that after reading this book you decide that you would still like to keep a budgerigar – or even several budgerigars – and that the information you have read will help you to keep fit, happy and healthy pets.

Useful Addresses

The Budgerigar Society
49/53 Hazelwood Road
Northampton NN1 1LG

Cage and Aviary Birds
Surrey House
1 Throwley Way
Sutton
Surrey SM1 4QQ

The Budgerigar Information Bureau
Stanhope House
Stanhope Place
London W2 2HH